T0159113

THE
DECISIONS
We Make

Gift on your: _____

From: _____

To: _____

ALSO BY THE AUTHOR

When Will Jesus Come?
Nigeria, 2004 (To be republished)

FORTHCOMING

The Severability Doctrine: *What will be must be*

THE
DECISIONS
We Make

THE PLACE OF GOD

This book is meant for all – Christians and non-Christians
alike, who are trying to make one decision or the other.
Before you finalize on that decision, read this book.

O. Ven Ogbebor

THE DECISIONS WE MAKE
THE PLACE OF GOD

Dominion Center
360 Elmhurst Road
Dayton OH 45417
(513) 503-0747
venovens@yahoo.com

iUniverse books may be ordered through booksellers or by contacting:

iUniverse
1663 Liberty Drive
Bloomington, IN 47403
www.iuniverse.com
1-800-Authors (1-800-288-4677)

ISBN: 978-1-5320-1497-0 (sc)
ISBN: 978-1-5320-1499-4 (hc)
ISBN: 978-1-5320-1498-7 (e)

Library of Congress Control Number: 2017902437

Print information available on the last page.

iUniverse rev. date: 03/15/2017

To my wife, IK.

To my children; Martin, Naomi, Osayi, and Odosa

ENDORSEMENTS

Pastor Ven Ogbebor with great passion, enthusiasm and love for mankind has skillfully brought into sharp focus a fundamental yet a very challenging human problem; Decision Making. In addition to his uncompromising analysis of the issues and problems concerning decision making, he also provided effective solutions. Irrespective of who and what we are, we make thousands of decisions every day. There are two basic types of decision; good and bad decisions. But how do we know that a good decision has been made? Pastor Ogbebor offered a solution. For a decision outcome to be congruent with the expected result when such decision was made, it must be aligned with the will of God and not our will. Whether you are a believer or not, this is a must read book. I recommend it

Dr. A. Osa. Obasogie.

A young man had gone visiting with an old man famed for his wisdom in search of the keys to success in life and business. "All you need to succeed in life and business is to know what to do next," the old man said. "And how do I know what to do next?" the young man asked. To this, the old man replied, "that is what you must figure out."

Pastor Ven Ogbebor, in this book, has graciously given us the master keys we need to "figure out what to do next." Our decisions make or mar us. Do you wish to make the right decisions all the time? Then read on!

'Tunde Fowe (Pastor, Teacher, Author and Family Coach)
Family Values Impact Charitable Trust.
Lagos, Nigeria.

ACKNOWLEDGEMENTS

In my spiritual journey, so far, certain groups of people have inspired me and the things I have done. I looked around and group these classes of people into five, not in any particular order.

Church of God Mission Int'l, Ekehuan Road branch, Benin City. Nigeria is where I started my spiritual journey as a new convert; that was where I rebooted my spiritual life, where my first book was launched, where I was given the opportunity to first hold a leadership position in the Christian race. Most of the foundational things I knew as a leader are the things I learnt as the youth president of this branch. I will forever remember the youths I led at that time, the youths with whom I worked in that branch, and those with whom I worked in the zone when I later became the youth zonal coordinator. They touched my life in every little way. Many of them are now founders of their own church ministries, and some have grown into leadership in other capacities. Thank you all.

My family that has supported me all the way. When you dream, and share your dream with your spouse and children, you are just bringing them into your dream. Ordinarily your dream doesn't bind them, but when they support you to bring your dream to reality, it is so much sacrifice because in so doing, they are giving up some privileges. To my wife and children, I recognize this and I say thank you with so much love.

To every member of The Redeemed Christian Church of God (RCCG) I have come to know in the United States and beyond, I say thank you for letting me serve you, for listening to me, for teaching me, and for letting me be a part of your family. You inspire me to accept a pastoral position which has further encouraged me in the work of the ministry. Thank you.

RCCG Dominion Center Dayton where I currently pastor. They received me as a co-laborer. They have encouraged me through difficult times, through hard and tough times, through rain and sunshine. I have not had any reason to regret becoming a pastor because the members are not just church members, but family members. To all of you, I say thank you.

To the individuals that have touched my life personally; my elder brother – my father, Mr. V. O. Ogbebor, Asst. Controller-General of Prisons (Rtd.) who God used to raise me; Bernard Ediagbonya, a brother who kept pooling me to the youth ministry at CGMi Ekehuan branch after my conversion; Barrister Nosa Ihaza, a friend that stuck closer than a brother in those early difficult days (who also help in editing this book); and to all very numerous people that have supported my ministry. I say thank you.

CONTENTS

FOREWORD

I have had the privilege of knowing and working with Pastor Ven Ogbebor for several years. Our church group, The Redeemed Christian Church of God, has afforded us the opportunity to minister to God's people and serve in this ever increasing vineyard. Pastor Ven is an anointed preacher and teacher of the word of God, with a passion to see people understand and enter into the fullness of God's desire for their lives. As the Coordinator over the area in which Pastor Ven serves, I have witnessed firsthand, his passion for people and his unique gifting in expounding the scriptures.

This book, "The Decisions We Make – The place of God" is timely and needed for every believer today. It focuses on a subject that tends to be overlooked and taken for granted, but is increasingly becoming a discipline that is lacking in the modern day believer.

Pastor Ven begins the book by evaluating the realities of our daily lives and how prayer, perseverance and faith in the word of God are necessities for every believer. He then proceeds to give practical insights on how to make decisions, both the everyday kind and the ones we make once or twice in a lifetime. When properly applied, these steps will help us avoid the pitfalls and regrets that result from poorly conceived decisions made without God as the center and pivot. I am confident that you will be blessed and enriched by this book.

F. Akin. Tella
Zonal Coordinator, Ohio Zone 2
The Redeemed Christian Church of God
North America

INTRODUCTION

Quite often, I have heard people exclaim "God! How did I miss it?" "As hard as I tried yet I failed," "How come everyone else is succeeding but when I try, my case is always different?" I have equally seen a lot of people giving up on a life-long dream because it is taking longer than they expected to achieve/realize. Some people have even totally erased the words "try harder" from their vocabulary because they believe they have tried the hardest. It's not coincidental that for some, at every point of success, they find out that they must start all over again. In Matthew 19:26, the bible says "Jesus looked at them and said, "With man this is impossible, but with God **all things** are possible." Therefore, in everything we have done that we didn't succeed, for every step we have taken that failed, for that dream that eventually died after we have tried so hard, there was something missing – GOD.

I have been there at some point where I had to ask myself "where did I go wrong?" The answer has always been "with God ALL things are possible." If you persist and don't give up, you will succeed at God's appointed time. (I addressed Persistence in this book).

Many people have taken God off their plans, hence the struggle and eventual failure. That is another reason for this book.

A lot of people pursue some careers because their friends are doing well in it, but they end up not continuing in that career because it turned out not to be what they expected. It's not surprising that some people have ideas about so many things; they even get some form of training in almost all of them, but they never master any of them. They never follow any till the end. This is because they were pursuing other people's dreams and not theirs.

At the tower of Babel in Genesis 11, the bible records that God saw the work that men did and He concluded that "If as one people speaking the same language they have begun to do this (building a tower they purpose in their heart to reach heaven), then nothing they plan to do will be impossible for them." God saw the power of unity and one language amongst men, I believe too that we will do greatly if we have that same kind of unity with God and speak His language.

If God's hands are in your business, you will not fail because God is not a failure. The bible says *"But seek ye first the kingdom of God, and his righteousness; and all these things shall be added unto you.- Matthew 6:33.*

If we put God first in the decisions we make; to raise a

family, to pursue a career, to establish a company, to make investments, the choice of whom to marry, even the choice of what to name your child, and type of car to buy etc., any decision at all that needs to be made, you will see the hand of God in it. Seek Him first, not later. Work and walk with Him, He will not leave you by yourself.

Chapter One
LIFE IS ROSY?

While it is our desire to go through life without a hitch, life does not present to us any of such opportunity; it may come but for a while.

There is the proverbial "born with the silver spoon." To many of the people who share this attribute, they may equally share, or at least act in the belief that life may be a bed of roses, but is life really all that?

Many people will differ, especially those that have seen the different faces and segments of all it can take to define what life is all about. Some people dwell in deception portraying to close allies and distant admirers who and what they really are not. Of a truth, there really lie some issues that need reconciliation.

While there are some perfect situations or perfect

1

moments, they don't last forever because everything is but for a while. We were admonished that trials will come, tribulations will come. We were also told that temptations will come; some are God-designed (Trials, Job 23:10), some by the devil (Temptations, Matthew 4:3-7). If you are trusted by God, He will allow you to be tempted by the devil (Matthew 4:1, Job 1:6-12) and if you remain steadfast, He will protect you and He will deliver you. God can try you, but only the devil tempts.

While it is our desire to go through life without hitches, life does not present to us any of such opportunity; it may come but for a while. What you do with such good moment matters, for it creates either a better next chance or a worse situation. No wonder it is said that "the rich also cry." For many people, converting to the Christian faith was or is a visualization of a future filled with hopes, filled with optimism, a brighter and better immediate future, a fantasy world where everything will fall in line at the snap of a finger. Shortly after conversion, there lies a realization of the unexpected. A new convert will begin to hear words like demon, enemy, principalities, powers, wickedness in high places, and so on. They will begin to grapple with the fact that to be able to overcome this unseen enemy, there are imaginary huddles that must be crossed. There will be words that need to be confronted, like prayers, fasting, perseverance, exercise of faith, patient, and the types many people would not like to hear, "the will of God," and "God's appointed time."

While it is expedient to do the work of Him that sent us – winning souls, it will be better to know that declaring our faith in Christ is like declaring to serve in the army of any nation. You automatically become an enemy of an enemy nation. In this case, you become a soldier for Christ therefore, an enemy of the devil. What do soldiers do in preparation for war? They train (fasting and prayers), they are equipped (bible), they are drafted (missions). The army has battle grounds designated, but for Christians, the spiritual realm and the universe is the battle ground. The appropriate time for the battle is nights and days. While there will be an end to the war of nations at some point, the war we fight as Christians is a continuous one for as long as the devil is still alive. But there is hope, which is the essence of this book. The bible says *"When a man's ways please the Lord, He makes even his enemies to be at peace with him."* Proverbs 16:7.

So, even though as Christians we have to face a common enemy, the devil and his cohorts, we are the victorious ones because God is always on our side, for *one with God is majority.* Unbelievers face the same battle, but they are like dried leaves that can be blown away on either direction because it neither has weight nor life in it. Which will you prefer, to fight with God on your side or to fight without God?

WHY PRAYERS, WHY FASTING?

A born again Christian that does not know how to pray exposes him/herself to grave danger. Prayer is the key, the master key that opens doors that no man can lock. And when it locks no man can open.

If God is a sovereign God, why do we still need to pray? Prayer is like communicating with someone- a friend, a relative, a colleague, a parent etc. Prayer is asking for something from another person who is the rightful owner of that which you desire, or the one who is in possession of it and positioned to give it. Prayer to God is a private, personal conversation made with intent to get a response, a divine response. Whether we pray or not, God knows our desire anyway, but he wants us to ask. In Luke 18, Jesus encouraged his disciples to always pray and not give up. Prayer is a direct line to God while saying it through Jesus Christ, who is our mediator- Hebrews 4:16. If we ask in the name of Jesus, it will be done. Jesus said:

> "And I will do whatever you ask in my name,
> so that the Father may be glorified in the Son.
> You may ask me for anything in my name, and
> I will do it."
>
> JOHN 14:13- 14

When we are in need sometimes, we go to our parent(s), a friend, a neighbor, a relative we trust that will not tell our business to other people, and ask for what we know that friend has that we need. Sometimes, we go in company of another who will help plead our case. Jesus is our impleader, he pleads on our behalf, but we have to say what we want God to do for us. It could also be telling Him our present situation, a predicament which of cause might have been brought about by the devil. We can tell God about our fears, our failures, our difficulties, our trials, what is causing us anxieties. Prayer is asking God to do for us what we cannot do for ourselves, and what friends and other people cannot do for us. Prayer is asking for the kinds of favor, gifts, benefits, protections and promotions that God granted the prophets of old, that we can relate to today.

If prayer is talking to God, why do we have to fast? What is fasting anyway?

Fasting is abstinence from food and/or drinks and other necessary pleasures of life as a sign of private and personal consecration to God. While I will not go into details about what fasting is in this book, it is a topic of its own that I need to dwell on in another book. But for a new convert, it is important to know, that fasting is a requirement in the Christian faith. There was a time in the bible when a certain sick person who was always having seizures was brought to Jesus Christ for healing. The disciples tried to heal him but could not. After Jesus healed him, the disciples wanted to know why they could not heal him. Jesus said in Matthew

17:21, "... *this kind does not go out except by prayer and fasting.*" There is a problem that prayers can solve but there are problems that need the combined efforts of fasting and prayers, and there is yet the kind that requires the combo effort of fasting and prayers done as a group, and that done as a whole church which is corporate intercession. Denying oneself of food and/or drink is for a higher benefit. Fasting can be done for the general good of the church, a church group, a family, on behalf of self and others etc.

Fasting could be done for a spiritual cleansing of the body, or of the land as it was the case in Nineveh after Jonah had told the people of Nineveh that God was going to destroy their land. They fasted, and so did their animals according to the Lord's instructions. And God had compassion on them.

THE PLACE OF PERSEVERANCE

Jesus said "*I have told you these things so that in me you may have peace. In the world you have trouble and suffering, but take courage — I have conquered the world.*" John 16:33. Many difficult times and troubles Christians face are by the design of this world. However, many are the result of people trying to adjust to the needs and standards of the society, and the world at large in trying to live according to the dictates of other people. As we grow in faith, sins are always around us;

in our thoughts, in our views/sight, in our actions, and in our conversations. Some are created by greed, a desire for self-satisfaction and the act of vengeance. As we struggle through these troubles, it is encouraging that there's hope of total salvation, but that is if the willingness for it is present.

Perseverance is remaining steadfast, trusting God as we go through these trials, knowing that with God, the end will come in our favor. Perseverance is trusting God through our present pains and difficulties, hoping with faith for a better tomorrow. Perseverance is the belief that God will perfect the work He started in us with our secured hope in His faithfulness.

Perseverance, which I see a little different from patience, is enduring the troubles and calamities, bad and difficult times or situations; uncertainties and commotion brought on us by the evils of other people, situations that we do not have control over but to watch as they unfold, which in most cases we do not envisage. Patience is simply waiting for an answer or a change in a situation that you have by yourself asked for either physically or in prayers. Perseverance is what Jesus experienced when he sensed that the hour has come, when he said;

> "Father, if you are willing, take this cup from
> me; yet not my will, but yours be done."
>
> LUKE 22:42

But the book of Matthew puts it this way;

> Going a little farther, he fell with his face to
> the ground and prayed, "My Father, if it is
> possible, may this cup be taken from me. Yet
> not as I will, but as you will."
>
> MATTHEW 26:39

This same prayer was said three times because he had no power over what was going to happen. He had to persevere. If it was something he had requested for, that he was patiently waiting for, he probably would have decided that he didn't want it any more.

As Christians, we persevere because Christ had told us that troubles will come but we should rejoice because he has overcome. In perseverance comes the exercise of faith, and the bible says in Hebrews 11:1 that faith is "...*the substance of things hoped for, the evidence of things not seen.*" It is belief that there's calmness in the midst of storm, not that there will be calmness; it is the belief in the existence of a solution even though it is not yet seen, and actual attainment of the next level where other people see barriers; it is the belief in the existence of life where others are seeing death; it is the belief in the resurrection of that business which everyone else is saying it's finished. That is faith. A proclamation as though a thing is in actual existence by believing that the power of God will bring it into existence.

I HAVE THE TOOLS, WHAT ARE MY EXPECTATIONS?

Prayer, fasting, faith, and perseverance are keys in the life of a new Christian convert. It is advised to know these, and do a personal tutoring to know the details. Ask your mentor, your group leader, your prayer partners, and even your pastor to aid you in any of these areas that you may find yourself lacking. We will face trials the moment we decide to serve God; the moment we decide to follow him; the moment we decide to join God's own army. Jesus Christ was not tempted until he was ready to launch his ministry after praying and fasting for forty days and forty nights. Temptation is not a one-time thing, it could come at the peak of that great revival you spent time, money, and energy preparing for. It could come when the doors of greatness are about to open. It could come at the hour of your breakthrough. Many ministers of the gospel have fallen at times like this and began to try to put the remainder of their once blossoming spiritual life back together. At some point, it gets too late. This is not by accident. Jesus said;

> "Behold, I send you forth as sheep in the midst
> of wolves; be ye therefore wise as serpents, and

harmless as dove. But beware of men: for they will deliver you up to the councils, and they will scourge you in their synagogues; And you shall be bright before governors and kings for my sake, for a testimony against them and the gentiles."

MATTHEW 10:16-18

Whichever way this passage is interpreted, it should be a guiding principle in all that we do, knowing that our adversary, the devil, is always at work. It may be that you just resumed at your new job which you love so much only to discover that your colleagues do not like you. In a situation as this, you are like a sheep in the midst of wolves; it may have to do with the contract you just won that now you are beginning to wonder why you even bided for it in the first place, because it's not working out; it may be in your new relationship that you have tried and sacrificed so much for, yet it's not working out; it could be one or some of your children falling into the deep that you have longed protected them from, thus bringing shame to the family; it could be in the ministry you prayerfully founded and nurtured that is now gradually folding up; or a career you have invested so much time and money into that has not yielded any dividend, and the possibility of it happening is not in sight; or health that suddenly began to fail due to no fault of yours. We can go on and on. In all these, remember that you can always trust in God, our dependable ally who said *"... Never will I leave you; never will I forsake you."* Hebrew 13:5. Has someone troubled you to the point where you begin to have sleepless nights? God says *"Be strong and courageous. Do not be afraid or terrified because of them, for the LORD your God goes with you; he will never leave you nor forsake you."* Deuteronomy 31:6.

The promises of God are not for a season, but from seasons to seasons which the bible described as in and out of season. *"No one will be able to stand against you all the days of your life,"* He says, *"As I was with Moses so I will be with you; I will never leave you nor forsake you."* Joshua 1:5.

New converts suffer castigation and ridicule in the hands of old friends, and some relations who still cannot fathom the fact that this veritable instrument (the new convert) has crossed over into the hands of God. They are called names; they are tempted by the things they used to love - drinking, smoking, clubbing, gambling, flirtatious living, scamming, falsification etc. Remain clinged unto God for there's rejoicing. Do not be moved.

> "And David said to his son, Solomon. Be strong
> and of good courage, and do it; do not fear nor
> be dismayed, for the Lord God – my God –
> will be with you. He will not leave nor forsake

you, until you have finished all the work for the service of the house of the Lord."

1 CHRONICLES 28:20

The word of the Lord is the hope of all believers. Depending on where you stand to telescope the situation, it is all rosy. If you decide to meditate upon the gossip of unbelievers; or on the threat that you received; or to dwell upon the report of those who have tried and failed before, trying to do what you are doing; or your personal inability to deal with certain situations, you may not believe in the possibility of turning around the situation because you may be dwelling in the negative. The Psalmist says *"Wait on the Lord: be of good courage, and he shall strengthen thine heart: wait, I say, on the Lord."* Psalm 27:14, and Proverbs 3:5 says *"Trust in the Lord with all your heart and lean not on your own understanding."* What then do you understand?

Not many Christians really have a clear idea of what it means to **understand the word of God**. Understanding simply means standing under the one who really knows, with a willingness and readiness to learn, and to follow the ways of such a one.

Let us look at the promises of God. Many, if not all promises of God are preconditioned, but most people pay attention to the promises and not the conditions. If you understand God, you will know that with God there is no accident, which means, nothing catches Him unaware. Everything, including bringing His promises concerning your life to pass, is all planned. If you desire to receive an income at the end of the day, or at the end of the week, or bi-monthly, or monthly as the case may be, you will need to work to gain that expectation of income. Even when you have done your part and it still doesn't seem to be working out, here comes the power of perseverance or patience, exercising your faith in God and His power to do, for there's nothing that happens under the heavens that God does not know about.

In 1 Thessalonian 5:18, we are admonished to *"give thanks in all circumstances, for this is God's will for you in Christ Jesus."* If it happens, it's because God approved of it. I lost my very first car when I was teaching a friend how to drive; he ran into a school wall. Many people expected him to pay for it and he was so much willing to at least make a contribution towards buying another car, but I was so unwilling to let him. When people asked me why, I simply told them I could have ran into a school bus on my way home after teaching him, I could have had an accident that will result in death or serious bodily injury, or simply could have been worse than hitting a school wall or losing a car. God let it happen to avert a more dangerous situation and so be it. The testimony that followed was that I got a better, and a bigger vehicle at my own price just for reciting John 3:16.

In Job chapter 1, the devil had to take permission from

God for him to tempt Job because God protected Job so much that the devil could not reach/touch him. God did not just protect him for nothing because even God Himself testified to it in Job 1:8 that he was a "perfect and an upright man, one that feared God and eschew evil." What qualities do you possess that will make God say for this reason, "I will build a hedge around you?" Working with God requires an understanding of the ways of God.

Understanding goes beyond 'a knowing.' Understanding is an in-depth knowledge, knowing beyond the surface. You knew your spouse by name the first time you met or started admiring him/her, but over time you got to understand that at certain times of the year he/she experiences some kinds of allergy; that he/she doesn't eat certain food; that things that excite you may freak him/her out; that he/she reacts to dreams in a different way than you do; that there are valuable deposits in him/her. When people are asked, for instance, to pray for the gifts of the spirit, for divine intervention, for spiritual maturity, for a visitation of the holy ghost etc., the prayer is usually colder and calmer than when you tell the congregation to pray for wealth, for increase all around, for expansion, for a new job, for promotion, for a life partner etc. This is because people understand what it means to be poor, what it means to be stagnant, what it means to be jobless, what it means to experience delays in life. Understanding God takes the same way. You don't understand God by reading John 3:16 once; but a reading of that passage over and over will broaden your understanding of whom God really is.

Therefore, now that you have the tools, your expectations are that they will be put into use. To be able to use the tools the opportunity must present itself. Well, that is in the sense of the world. In the Christian race the opportunity opens the day you become born again. That is why we should always be prepared. 1 Thessalonian 5:17 says *"Pray without ceasing."* If you are in a battle field, you don't fight one day and take the other day off. The bible says;

"For the weapons of our warfare are not carnal, but mighty through God for the pulling down of strong holds."

2 CORINTHIANS. 10:4

Our weapons are meant for a purpose (pulling down of strong holds). What are strong holds anyway? I will explain some of them. There is a weakness in a man's life (man in the generic usage), e.g. alcoholism. An alcoholic doesn't take his eyes off alcoholic drinks so long as he has money to buy it, or so long as it is offered to him. Many times he has taken the decision to change his lifestyle, but just at that point, he gets exposed to free drinks and opportunities to get them at will, then he changes his mind again. Drinking has kept him away from changing his lifestyle, from becoming born again. That is the devil's strong hold in his life. It is the same for a drug addict, a thief, a liar, a smoker, a prostitute, an adulterous person, a fornicator, a cheat etc. All are the same, depending on what your weakness is. It is stronghold because it's a situation you just can't let go each time you try. But the good news is that with your weapons of prayer, fasting, exercise of faith, it is possible. God has made those weapons mighty for you to be able to pull down those strong holds in your life.

Your expectations therefore include the fact that situations will arise where you will need to put your weapons into use. Persecution: yes, you will be persecuted. People that know your old ways and approved of it will call you names. They will try to rubbish you just to see if you are really whom you say you are (your new faith). They will tempt you no matter how long it takes. A certain pastor who dedicated his life to the work of God soon had a breakthrough in his ministry, a lot of people were pouring into his services and soon had to split into multiple services. On Sundays, people would fall down at the sound of his voice, God was healing people by him laying hands on them, things were happening and miracles were taking place. As membership grew so was the need for workers. Among the people that volunteered to work for the church was an extra ordinarily dedicated lady who was always ahead of the game; she maintained the pastor's appointments and schedules, guest speakers' welfare, church meetings' schedules, etc. One Sunday after service, she was among the few people that stayed behind as usual until everybody else left. She and the pastor went over some tidying ups as usual and then the unexpected happened. The pastor slept with her. The lady got up and said "yes, this was my mission." The pastor said at that point his eyes became open and realized how the devil has used that lady against him and his ministry.

Every one of us has a strong hold, it may not be as bad as that of the pastor, it could be the smallest things as too tired to pray, cheating in a game, signing the wrong time on attendance sheet at work, manipulating figures in account books, etc., it is all because there is a strong hold. Prayers can help, fasting can help, exercising faith that with God breaking such strong hold is possible. That is what they are meant for. Every manipulation of the power of darkness, evil machinations, the target of principalities and powers, all manifest in these strong holds. They need to be pulled down. Prayers and fasting can do it if you believe.

Temptations to sin are bound to happen; persecution will come, trials and tribulations will come, there will be delays in life sometimes, certain kinds of denial will happen, disappointments and rivalry will be there, that is why Jesus said "I have told you these things so that in me you may have peace. In the world, you have trouble and suffering, but take courage – I have conquered the world." John 16:33. This means that though these things are there, if you hold onto God steadfastly, you will overcome. In fact, the New International Version of the bible aptly puts the above passage this way;

> "I have told you these things, so that in me you may have peace. In this world you will have trouble. But take heart! I have overcome the world
>
> JOHN 16:33

It is possible to find a Christian who knows and has his/her weapons, knows his/her expectations, does almost everything right, but yet, things still go wrong. Why? That is the purpose of this book; to address the decisions we make, how we arrived at those decisions, and the repercussion(s) — reward or punishment.

Chapter Two

WHERE DID I GO WRONG?

It's possible to know when situation became worse, if we sometimes stop in the midst of so much craziness to re-examine ourselves, and our situation.

WHAT MUST GUIDE OUR DECISIONS

I write this book believing that I will be addressing believers, but if you are not, glory be to God that this is an opportunity knocking at your door for you to become one. I encourage you to open your heart to accept Jesus Christ as your Lord and personal savior, as the son of God who died in your place in order for you to have access to the living king, the almighty God.

Once upon a time, there lived a man who was so dedicated

to his farm work; he did everything that could reasonably be done to have not just great expectation but to actually realize his expectations of a great harvest. This was the practice every year, and his harvest never fell short of that expectation until that year. He has done all that needed to be done as always, but that year, his harvest was the poorest. As everyone wondered what could have happened, his question was "where did I go wrong?"

You may have at one point or the other experienced situations like that in your live, where you asked similar questions about event(s) happening around you, either caused by you or being in a position where you have to suffer the consequence; it may be a test you studied so hard for but failed it; you work multiple jobs but you're still unable to catch up with your bills; very dutiful and hardworking at your job but the promotions keep passing you by; very diligent in living a trouble-free life but family members keep inviting troubles; you have lived right, eaten right, but suddenly began to experience health failure; you have been trained in various careers but none has been able to fetch you a good and desired job etc. We can go on and on. While it might not necessarily be your fault, sometimes, it may be. Thus, the Apostle Paul admonished us not to:

> Worry about anything; instead, pray about everything. Tell God what you need, and thank him for all he has done."
>
> PHILIPPIAN 4:6

Let us look at the four parts to the above scripture which most of the time people don't consider in making decisions. It starts with an advice, *"Do not worry about anything."* But we do worry about everything. When Jesus was teaching his disciples how to pray in the book of Matthew, he asked them to ask for anything one day at a time – *"Give us this day our daily bread,"* Matthew 6:11. But are we really able to worry about one day at a time? If we do, we won't have a savings and retirement accounts; we won't have a refrigerator in our homes; we will not need to have many different kind of clothes and shoes; we will not even need to have anything that will last for more than a day. But what Jesus Christ was saying was that we should not be too carried away about the things of tomorrow instead of taking care of one another TODAY. Simply put, if you are satisfied with today, endeavor to positively affect the life of another who is in need instead of piling up for tomorrow like the rich fool in Luke chapter 12.

1. Do not Worry about Anything

Things happen to believers for a reason, but we are consoled with the fact that nothing happens under the earth that God does not know about, including that your situation. God is all-knowing, which means He knows everything. He alone sees the end from the beginning. If your speed is too fast for

Him to take control of your situation, He can slow you down or even stop you. If you appear "too busy" to listen to Him when He needs to send you on an errand, He can slow you down or stop you as He did to Jonah when He caused Jonah to be swallowed by the Whale when Jonah was running away from going to Nineveh as God has instructed.

God can stop you from moving forward or slow you down when there's an imminent danger ahead of you. You just got new set of tires and you embarked on a journey when in the middle of your journey you had a flat tire. It is possible that the prayers you said before leaving the house is working for you because God just protected you from a motor accident that would have involved you.

God can relocate you for safety reasons, and He can reposition you for a blessing too. No matter the situation you find yourself, give Him thanks. If you are a faithful servant of God, He can alter your plans for a better tomorrow. He can force anyone to do His will even if it's not convenient. Looking back at the story of Jonah, the bible records that "*the Lord provided a great fish to swallow Jonah, and Jonah was inside the fish three days and three nights,*" Jonah 1:17. This was done for the will of God to be carried out. If you prayed about your situation and believed that God has taken control, also believe that whatever has made you ask "where did I go wrong?" is the great fish that has been meant to swallow you. It is a time to stop and think, reboot, and reconnect with God. The situation is not meant to kill you, but to slow you down for the will of God to be perfected in your life concerning that situation.

When Paul instructed the Philippian church not to worry about anything, he was speaking the true illustration of himself, emphasizing what he himself had experienced. Many people think that the accumulation of wealth is what secures their tomorrow, Jesus warned us in Luke 12 when he spoke about the rich fool:

> "Watch out! Be on your guard against all kinds of greed; life does not consist in an abundance of possessions." And he told them this parable: "The ground of a certain rich man yielded an abundant harvest. He thought to himself, 'What shall I do? I have no place to store my crops.' "Then he said, 'This is what I'll do. I will tear down my barns and build bigger ones, and there I will store my surplus grain. And I'll say to myself, "You have plenty of grain laid up for many years. Take life easy; eat, drink and be merry.'" But God said to him, 'You fool! This very night your life will be demanded from you. Then who will get what you have prepared for yourself?' "This is how

it will be with whoever stores up things for themselves but is not rich toward God."

LUKE 12:15-21

GOD STILL SPEAKS

Many times, it's possible to know when things started going wrong. It's possible to know when situation became worse if we can only stop in midst of so much craziness to re-examine ourselves, and our situation. When things change suddenly and take the down turn where there was no apparent wrong doing (sin), then believe that God is trying to get your attention, or pass an information across to you. Many people don't believe that God still speaks, but the last time I checked, He is still the same God who spoke to Abraham to leave his father's house to a place He would show him; the same God who spoke to Moses to go and confront Pharaoh; the same God of David, Solomon, Elijah, Elisha, Isaac, Jacob, and all the great prophets of old. He has never changed, and will never change. He's not a dumb God, He still speaks. People these days don't hear Him because they are too engrossed and carried away by the things of this world. Technological advancement has not helped either.

Today, people spend so much time on Instagram, Facebook, Twitter, LinkedIn, Google, YouTube etc., trying to see who liked and/or commented on their pictures, who commented on their posts and what they said, responding to people's reactions about posts, and before you know it, they have spent eight hours on their phone, tablet, IPad, computer, or laptop. When you spend eight hours surfing and browsing and talking on the phone, and another six to eight hours of sleep, coupled with about two hours for three meals and snacks, you will suddenly discover that twenty-four hours are not enough in a day any more. To so many people, they do elimination series to take away the less important activities from their schedule; unfortunately, God and the things of God are always the first to be considered. That is why it's so convenient for "believers" to choose to work extra hours on Sunday mornings believing that pastor will understand, but they forget that they are not accountable to the pastor who himself is running his own race. May God help us in Jesus name.

God still speaks if we care to listen. A man with an ear piece in his ear, and a phone in his hand, is waiting for the next call and not to hear the voice of God. The bible encourages us to watch and pray, but it depends on what you are watching. When you pray, it depends on where you are expecting your answers from. Many indulge so much in sinful acts that they don't know what sin is anymore. Even when God speaks to them, they push it into their subconscious mind.

The rich fool did not count it as sin for him to be storing

up food for his "soul to eat and be merry," or maybe he knew and totally disregarded it. In Judges 16:1-21, Samson ignored the fact that he committed sin when he slept with Delilah, the prostitute, and later fell at her lap who tried three times to take away the source of his strength. Samson should have known better to move on without Delilah, but he didn't. Would it have been okay for Samson to ask "where did I go wrong" when calamity befell him? He sure knew where he went wrong. It is said that a dog that is ready to get lost does not listen to his master's whistle. God gave Samson opportunities to know that he was dining with the devil but Samson just refused to hear, an act that led to his eventual death.

In all our struggles, there is a Delilah (the strong hold I discussed earlier); and in all our life's journeys, there are storms. But in all these there's God. He will always make out a way where we think there is none if only we are willing and ready to obey Him and follow His leading.

When God appeared unto Solomon and asked him to make a request, Solomon requested for wisdom, God said to him; "*behold, I have done **according to your words**. Behold, I have given you a wise and discerning heart, so that there has been no one like you before you, nor shall one like you arise after you.*" 1 Kings 3:12. God has given us wisdom to deal with every of our situations only if we recognize His power.

2. PRAY ABOUT EVERYTHING

Prayer is the key that can open every spiritually closed doors. In any decision we make, let us try to always submit it first in prayers before the Lord - the choice of a life partner, the career we need to pursue, the place to permanently reside, the area we need to serve in the house of God, even the decision of which church to make a home church. Seek the face of God, and ask Him to lead the way, for whomever God leads never misses his/her way. As Christians, we are encouraged to *"pray without ceasing"* 1 Thessalonians 5:17. There's nothing we can do by ourselves that will materialize as expected without prayers. You may say some non-Christians succeed in their ventures while some Christians don't, which is true. But in such ventures Christians do better, and even if not, our wealth is not measured by the amount of money we have, but by how much peace we have with God.

Once upon a time, there lived a very rich man who was so wealthy in the eyes of men, but he had no peace because of the source of his wealth. His wealth was acquired by entering into a demonic covenant which placed a limit on his number of years in life. Thinking at the time of the covenant that the number of years given him was long, he agreed. But before he knew it the years were running out, and he began to live in fear. He eventually died, his wealth wasted away because none of his children could manage it (of course it was not real). It is better to drink a glass of water and have peace with God than to feast at a buffet and spend the whole night sobering.

Psalm 145:18 says *"The LORD is near to all them that call on him, to all that call on him in truth."* If you pray in truth believing in God, He will answer you. But you have a role to play; you have to call on Him, and you have to call on Him in truth. It is true that God knows every of our situations, and even when you kneel to pray He already knows what you are about to ask, but He requires us to ask (call), and believe truly in Him, that is, believing in his power to do. In addition to believing, you must be sure to do away with sin because God cannot behold sin neither can He stand the sight of a sinner. The bible says in Proverbs 15:29 that *"The LORD is far from the wicked: but he hears the prayer of the righteous,"* If you want God to be close to you, to hear you when you call, you have to give up your wicked ways. You must be righteous.

Occasional or ceremonial prayers are not enough, but praying about everything and at all times. The book of 1 Peter 5:8 admonishes that we should *"Be sober, be vigilant, because your adversary the devil walketh about as a roaring lion, seeking whom he may devour."* No animal goes to sleep knowing that the lion is roaming around the neighborhood, hungry. The devil, like the roaming lion, does not sleep neither does he rest. If he doesn't rest, we are advised not to, but to always pray. In the time of sleep the enemies are at work.

"But while men slept, his enemy came and sowed tares among the wheat, and went his way."

MATTHEW 13:25

In our moments of prayerlessness, the enemies are still at work trying to harm/hurt us. The enemies will still be stealing our joy and causing us damages and piling up defeat against us. But with God, we can defeat them with our prayers.

"The thief cometh not, but for to steal, and to kill, and to destroy: …"

JOHN 10:10

Our moment of wondering where we went wrong is the moment where our enemy steals our joy by making us meet with disappointments. Our inability to handle such situations may escalate to a moment of 'a killing' which may eventually lead to destruction. It is important we recognize that God sees our situations in times of difficulties, temptations, and trials. A person who meets with disappointment and not holding on to God may decide to stop going to church, may decide to stop praying, may decide to take an easy route to fix it. In doing so he gets himself deeper into a mess which may be taking him farther away from God, and anyone who is not with God is set for destruction. You cannot sit on the fence either.

> "No man can serve two masters: for either he will hate the one, and love the other; or else he will hold to the one, and despise the other. Ye cannot serve God and mammon."
>
> MATTHEW 6:24

It is important to pray about everything and at every time, and everywhere; before we go to bed, immediately we wake up, before we eat, before leaving the house, before starting to plan any program or event, before and after every meeting, in times of celebrations and in times of adversity, before and after every examination/test, in times of gain and in times of loss, at birth and at death, when hired or fired, in sickness and in health, in times of decision making, whether rich or poor, etc. There is need to pray at all times so that the devil will not have access point into our lives.

3. TELL GOD WHAT YOU NEED

Prayer is a communication between individuals or group of people and God. Prayer, like a discussion with our earthly parents, friends, neighbors, pastor, church members, colleagues etc., is directed at God. For Christians, it is a direct line to heaven, through Jesus Christ. Adherents to other religions pray too but that is not the focus of this book. In praying as Christians, we are talking to God about our needs, our desires, our challenges and difficulties, and trials. In prayers, we can also appreciate God for what He has done for us. In prayers, we can confess our sins and ask for forgiveness. In prayers, we make vows to do or not to do. In prayers, we can highlight our expectations but we must be ready and willing to accept the will of God.

As noted above, it is necessary to pray at all times – talking to God. We have to tell Him about that meeting we are about to start, about that examination/test that we are about to take, or just taken. We have that privilege to talk to God about everything and anything. It is a privilege because a lot of people wish they can pray even though they believe in God. Believers talk to God and unbelievers equally have the right to talk to God but the difference is that there is hope for believers for "... *Christ in us, the hope of glory.*" Colossians 1:27.

As Christians, we talk to God with a heart of expectation that when we ask, God will give to us our demands and desires according to His will, but we must TALK to Him. Jesus said about when we ask, that he;

> "will do whatever you ask in my name, so that
> the Father may be glorified in the Son. You

may ask me for anything in my name, and I
will do it."

JOHN 14:13-14

And Paul gave the assurance that when we ask, God will
provide for ALL our needs according to His riches in glory,
which means, you may not get everything exactly the time you
asked for it, or in the exact way you intended, but he will grant
it at a time that is appropriate and in a better form. *"But my
God shall supply all your needs according to his riches in glory by
Christ Jesus."* Philippians 4:19.

Christians struggle with the belief that God is sometimes
slow in answering prayers, what we should understand is that
God does not work in accordance with our timing, neither is
He subjected to our own calendar. The bible says He makes
everything perfect (beautiful) in its time (Ecclesiastes 3:11).
Whatever comes to you at the time you need it is at a perfect
time, if it does not, still give God the praise for He alone
knows the best, but you still need to ask and believe.

4. THANK GOD FOR ALL HE HAS DONE

In every situation, we are admonished to always give God
thanks. We cannot see what He averts on our behalf, but
He will do it even if it means denying us of some personal
gratifications. We should always have the heart of thanksgiving

because He planned for us to succeed and not to fail. Whenever we experience "failure", God may be saying it is not yet time to get to the next level. It's possible He wants to prepare us some more for a level higher than we are asking for. But in every little thing, let's acknowledge God's hands and give Him thanks. His word says;

> "Whoever can be trusted with very little can also be trusted with much, and whoever is dishonest with very little will also be dishonest with much."
>
> LUKE 16:10

There is a popular saying that one good turn deserves another. If you thank God for what He has done for you, your family, concerning your health, your job, your finances, even for the gift of life, He is well and able to do more. But let Him know you appreciate the air you breathe, the sun that shines, even for the rain. The book of 1 Thessalonians 5:18 says *"In everything give thanks: for this is the will of God in Christ Jesus concerning you."* Which means we cannot pick and choose when to thank God, and under what situation.

There is always something to thank God for if we have a heart of appreciation. Often times, people look at their situations and think God has not done well enough for them compared to what He has done for their friends, their neighbors, their colleagues, for other family members, but think about how many people you have known that are no more, but you are still alive. Think about that person who is surviving by buying oxygen but you are not. Think about how many people that are homeless but you are not. Think about the number of job losses monthly but you have always had a job, sometimes two or even three jobs. Think about the number of people that do not have a family but you always have family members around you. We can go on and on. There is a need to appreciate God. You might not be where you want to be today but you are not where you were yesterday. Life is work in progress, a journey in which only God guarantee our tomorrow and our destination. If you have life, it's an opportunity to say "thank you Jesus for giving me another chance." Many sleep and they don't wake, some wake but they have their legs hung up on the hospital bed, some wish they could talk. A sincere heart will know that though they have not arrived, but there are many that want to get to where they are.

Thanking God is an attitude that can be developed and mastered. Learning to say "thank you " at all times will help develop this attitude when you see the hands of God in every of your situation. He watches over you; He cares for you. Whatever concerns you concerns Him. He can touch your situations too.

"For the eyes of the Lord run to and fro throughout the whole earth, to shew himself strong in the behalf of them whose heart is perfect toward him.

2 CHRONICLES 16:9

He heals our diseases, and sets us free from every sickness by His spoken word. He keeps us safe in times of trouble.

"He sent his word, and healed them, and delivered them from their destructions."

PSALM 107:20

Develop the attitude of trusting God and not worrying about everything. Develop the attitude of prayers, and praying about every situation. Develop the attitude of telling God about all you need and trusting Him to do what is best for you. Develop the attitude of thanking God for all He has done even if you don't see it, for we cannot really see everything God has done and will continue to do for us. Paul says;

"... Eye hath not seen, nor ear heard, neither have entered into the heart of man, the things which God hath prepared for them that love him."

1 CORINTHIANS 2:9

In so doing, our decisions are guarded, trusting that the good Lord will lead us right, and in the right direction. The decision we take can either make or break us. Therefore, it is important to bring God into our thoughts, our actions, and our spiritual life in order to be able to make the right decisions, and take the right steps.

Chapter Three

DECISIONS...
WHAT TO CONSIDER

We all get tempted at one point or the other, but if we have the fear of God, with a determination to shame the devil, we will overcome.

Many decisions we make/take are mostly premeditated. Thank God for the spirit of discernment which God has given to those who hear Him. It is the responsibility of every Christian to strive to be able to discern between good and evil. The bible says *"But examine everything carefully; hold fast to that which is good; abstain from every form of evil."* 1 Thessalonians 5:21-21. Apostle John issues a similar injunction when he admonishes us not to *"believe every spirit, but **test the spirits*** *to see whether they are from God; because many false prophets have gone out into the world."* 1 John 4:1. According to the New Testament, discernment is not optional for the believer, it is required.

The spirit of God dwells in every believer, and those who fear God. There are two sides to any decision; (1.) to do or not to do (2.) to do now or wait till later. At every critical point of decision making there is that still voice in our head that tends to tell us the right thing to do, but there is also the louder one which, in many cases, is deceiving. This stage is critical, which is why we need the power of the holy spirit to make such decisions. However, before we get to that stage there is a preconceived decision which we hope and believe will be the ultimate decision. When this does not turn out as expected, many people will still go ahead anyway which leads to what I call spiritual falsehood. Take a man that wants to steal for instance, he already made up his mind but decided to think about it. At this point, he's fighting whether or not to do it. A stronger and louder voice will say "Do it" and he jumps on it. There is also that still voice that says "Don't!", but that still voice is suppressed. As Christians, we should let the word of God direct and lead us at difficult times in terms of decision-making.

A person who already decided on what to do before going to a counselor may not deem the counselor as friendly if the counselor did not counsel along the line of his/her decision.

The same way people doubt the voice of God when God speaks to them concerning their prayer request, because the voice does not speak in line with their expectations.

Though we know most times that what we are doing or about to do is wrong, why then do we still do it? Many people think they are hiding where they cannot be seen, I tell you, you cannot hide from your shadow. It will bear witness against you on the last day. We know certain actions violate the law and that there's no way we can escape punishment if caught, yet we still engage in it anyway. We know that certain works, acts, speeches and concepts constitute sin, and knowing that *"the soul that sins MUST die,"* Ezekiel 18:20, *"For the wages of sin is death,"* Romans 6:23, why continue with the plan? James answers this question this way;

> "But each person is tempted when he is lured and enticed by his own desire. Then desire when it has conceived gives birth to sin, and sin when it is fully grown brings forth death."
>
> JAMES 1:14-15

In examining where we go wrong in making certain decisions, we will examine the above passage in three parts.

EACH PERSON IS TEMPTED WHEN HE IS LURED AND ENTICED BY HIS OWN DESIRE

Temptation and/or enticement has a major role to play when it comes to making certain decisions. Be it a decision regarding a particular job, the choice of a spouse (life partner), the decision on a course of study, the decision on the type of house to rent or to buy, the choice of a home church, the choice of the kind of car to buy or whether to even buy one etc.; it even goes further to whether or not to commit a particular sin, whether or not to commit to a church group, whether or not to take a ministerial assignment in the church or to say certain things etc. In Judges 16:4, the bible records that "some time later, he (Samson) *fell in love* with a woman in the Valley of Sorek whose name was Delilah." Samson's love for Delilah was his enticement, such as the things we either stand to gain or the satisfaction we tend to derive from our action. This desire, when pursued in a very vigorous way can block every of our sense of good judgment. The preacher may preach against it, a prophet may come to you to advise against it, God may even make you dream about it and to see the negative result of your action, all will be pushed down into the subconscious mind. It stays there till you achieve your desire, and then begin to blame the devil.

Samson desired in his heart in Judges 16:1 to mingle with a prostitute. Three times he had opportunities to walk away from Delilah but he will not because he had a desire to fulfill. Light and darkness have no business together.

> "Be ye not unequally yoked together with unbelievers: for what fellowship hath righteousness with unrighteousness? and what communion hath light with darkness?
>
> 2 CORINTHIANS 6:14

Samson's encounter with Delilah was an opportunity for him to retrace his steps but he didn't.

It is needful of us to know what our desires are, and what God wants of us. It is equally important to be able to strike a balance between the things we desire and the things we really need versus the will of God for us. Quite often, people will insist on God granting their desires because that is what He promised in Mark 11:24 "*Therefore I say unto you, what things soever ye desire, when ye pray, believe that ye receive them, and ye shall have*". They do this without regard as to whether or not what they desire is the will of God. An ungodly desire often meets with disappointments and regrets, but the will of God does not bring pain and suffering. The word of God says "*The blessing of the LORD maketh rich, and he addeth no sorrow with it.*" Proverbs 10:22. A struggle to fulfill our desire without bringing God into it often time leads to mistakes that could leads to worse situations. Samson's desire to have

Delilah made him to open his mouth and reveal the secrets of the source of his strength; it did not just end in him losing his strength but ended in his death, and yet he still lost Delilah.

The Israelites went to war to take Jericho in Joshua chapter 6. They were warned not to touch any of the "accursed things" which is something "under the ban" and marked for utter destruction, even though they were warned that taking any of those things will mean bringing a curse upon themselves and **the whole of Israel**. But what did Achan do? To satisfy his desire, he took from the accursed things and for this, Israel suffered defeat in the hands of a smaller army. Note here that even though it was Achan that stole from the accursed things, the entire nation was held liable for it. God said:

> "Israel hath sinned, and they have also transgressed my covenant which I commanded them: for they have even taken of the accursed thing, and have also stolen, and dissembled also, and they have put it even among their own stuff. Therefore, the children of Israel could not stand before their enemies, but turned their backs before their enemies, because they were accursed: neither will I be with you any more, except ye destroy the accursed from among you. Up, sanctify the people, and say, sanctify yourselves against tomorrow: for thus saith

the Lord God of Israel. There is an accursed
thing in the midst of thee, O Israel: thou canst
not stand before thine enemies, until ye take
away the accursed thing from among you."

JOSHUA 7:11-13

Achan, like Samson, like many of us, was tempted when
he was lured and enticed by his own desire to take from the
accursed things. Did he know that what he was doing was
wrong? Of course, he knew. But the enticement was something
he could not resist. The negative voice was louder and clearer
because he had purposed to take some of those things. He
could not resist the temptation. I'm sure the soft and still
voice was telling him too not to take, the voice must have
reminded him of the instruction not to take, but he chose to
follow his desire and brought punishment to a whole nation.
Many people are caught in this type of web. If you are, the
grace of God is available unto you for deliverance, and for the
spirit of discernment.

Idleness can sometimes make people take the wrong
decision. There is a saying that an idle mind is the devil's
workshop. An idle person has got lots of time to think of so
many things, including ungodly thoughts. Once an idea has
been thought about for a while, the desire to achieve it sets in.
Some people can control their desires and bring them under
the subjection of the holy spirit, but so many cannot. For

those that cannot discern a godly desire from an evil desire, it's more likely that they will end in doom unless they utilize their second chance of repentance.

There was a man in the bible, whose name was David. The bible records that when *"it was the time that kings go to war,"* David sent his men to war to fight the Ammonites but he decided to stay at home in Jerusalem (Wrong decision). At some points later, he decided to climb the roof of his house and take a look around his palace. Coincidentally, that was the time when a lady called Bathsheba was bathing in her own bathroom, and out of everything that surrounded the king's palace, all David could see was Bathsheba having her bath. David purposed in his heart to have her and he followed that desire through even though he was told whose wife she was. He would not listen because of an evil desire. 2 Samuel 11:1-5.

We all get tempted at one point or the other, but if we have the fear of God with a determination to shame the devil, we will overcome. Jesus Christ was tempted three times in Matthew chapter 4 at the point he was ready to launch out his ministry. Jesus would have been enticed by the benefit that the devil was offering. As hard as the devil tried to lure him into accepting the offer, Jesus Christ refused to be enticed and lured.

Samson is an example of someone who was lured – pressured to given up an entitlement. David is an example of a person that was enticed – caught in the web of that which creates a desire. Jesus Christ is an example of one who experienced both an enticement and a luring, but he prevailed.

Someone with a determination to attain or achieve certain desires will neglect every godly advice and counsel; even if the holiest person speaks to that fellow to help him realize the end result of that desire which will be a disaster. In Genesis 19, Lot's eldest daughter, while drawn with the desire to preserve their father's lineage got their father drunk and lured her younger sister into them sleeping with their father - Genesis 19:30-36. If they were convinced that what they were doing was right, would they have bothered getting their father drunk? I don't think so.

THEN EVIL DESIRE WHEN IT IS CONCEIVED GIVES BIRTH TO SIN

Desire, like a pregnant woman, knows what an outcome may be, though it could be sometimes wrong or beyond expectations. It is like a journey, until you arrive at your destination you are still journeying. Desire is what you purposed to achieve by your action, it is the end of a reason for an action; the ultimate goal for doing what you do whether good or bad. When there is conception, there's a delivery unless miscarriage occurs which is likened to aborting a desire or a plan. It takes the grace of God to abort an ungodly desire. Most times, an ungodly desire gives birth to sin, but when a child of God harkens to the voice of God and retracts, that ungodly desire is killed. It is aborted.

To conceive a desire goes beyond the desire itself; the ways to achieving that desire are carefully thought through, just like David did not stop at desiring to have Bathsheba, he sent for her to be brought, and after fulfilling the desire he thought of how to get rid of Uriah, her husband, so that he can permanently own her. Doesn't this sound like the stories we hear these days?

To achieve a desire requires planning, but no matter how much we plan God listens and sees the heart of the conceiver. God is sometimes referred to as the silent listener to every conversation. He has given us the spirit to be able to discern good from evil, it is at this point you put that spirit to work on your behalf. If you perceive it's evil and you are determined to make heaven, flee! The bible admonishes us to *"abstain from every form of evil"* some versions say *"Abstain from all **appearance** of evil."* 1 Thessalonians 5:22. Once you think about it, call upon the name of God and ask the Holy Spirit to guard you. The best point at which to reject evil thought is the best time to abort a devilish desire, and it is right from the point of the initial thought. Do not wait to see if you can resist it later, do not try to pretend to concede for a while. Do not even walk away or run away, the bible say FLEE! By the time you go from conceiving an ungodly act and following through with planning, and arriving at the concluding part of the matter (the desire), the heart would have been filled already; too full to resist the temptation.

Conceiving a desire starts with a temptation – a ploy by the devil to rubbish, to bring down, to destroy a God-fearing person, to contend with God as he did in the case of Job in Job Chapter 1. The person tempted only sees the "good" part of the desire, and until the end is achieved there is no going back. People lie to gain favor, to be comfortable, to have a place in their peer group, to look nice. Some people lie to cause another person anger. People cheat to gain promotion or satisfaction, to undo another emotionally. People take short cuts to get by faster. Some people kill to achieve a devilish intention, or to cover up a past occurrence, or an illegal purpose. Some will deceive in other to take from the owners what rightfully belongs to them.

A DESIRE LACED WITH TEMPTATIONS

Temptation itself has a magnetic force that is used by only the devil or those whom the devil has purposed to use. The person being used by the devil must have given him/herself up to be used, which in itself is a concession to the temptation. Temptation is so magnetic that it draws or pulls a victim to itself in such a way and manner that s/he cannot either determine between right or wrong, or simply cannot just ignore it. But the good thing is that if you have God and you have the spirit of discernment, sometime even with strong moral upbringing, you will be able to discern that this is the devil's ploy. God has given us the power to say NO! and refuse to be used. Anyone used by the devil is a servant of the devil for we cannot serve two masters at the same time. The bible says *"No man can serve two masters: for either he will hate the one, and love the other; or else he will hold to the one, and despise the other. Ye cannot serve God and mammon."* Matthew 6:24.

The devil can also use someone else to get at you to perform an evil act; such as family members used to convince Christians to carry out unholy purposes – Job's wife told Job to curse God and die - Job 2:9. Job could have said well, since my wife said it it's probably okay. On King Herod's birthday, his wife, Herodias, used her daughter to get King Herod to chop off the head of John the Baptist whom she hated because John the Baptist had told the king that it was wrong to marry his brother's wife. Mark 6:17-28. The bible says *"My son, if sinners entice thee, consent thou not."* Proverbs 1:10. Some temptations may be difficult to overcome, but with God, all things are possible.

"No temptation has overtaken you that is not common to man. God is faithful, and he will not let you be tempted beyond your ability, but with the temptation he will also provide the way of escape, that you may be able to endure it.

CORINTHIANS 10:13

Permit me to say that we do not walk into temptation, temptation only presents itself. No one purposes in his or her heart that he/she wants to be tempted; but temptation to an unbeliever is seen as an opportunity because of its expected gain/benefit(s).

A seminary teacher once defined temptation as "the work of the devil to drag you to Hell!" Indeed, that is quite plain. Of course he went on to give more academic definitions when he said when battling temptation, we are in a war, a war with an enemy who wants to destroy us. He wants this because he is envious of the excellency of God. Temptation is an internal manifestation of an external influence; a presentation of an unsolicited, inexplicable, and unmerited favor; unexplained anticipated benefit that could be sometimes controllable, but most times, not controlled. Temptation is the presentation of an unholy and ungodly opportunity. To overcome it, we must submit to God for help. We cannot do it on our own if we rely on our ability. The bible says *"Submit yourselves therefore to God. Resist the devil, and he will flee from you."* James 4:7.

A temptation can be averted though it will always present itself. A newly married young man who left his newly wedded wife in the car and ran into the store to quickly get a surprise birthday gift was attracted by another young beautiful lady while he was in the store. The best thing at that time was to not get distracted, otherwise, a smile and a giving of attention, trying to gain acquaintance may lead to an unexpected end. In Genesis chapter 39, Joseph was tempted when the devil presented him with what some people will regard as "ample opportunity" to sleep with his master's wife. Joseph refused. Temptation came to Joseph but there also came deliverance, Joseph chose the latter to glorify the name of the Lord. The same temptation came upon King David when, despite everything that surrounded his palace, all he could see was a married woman having her bath in her own bathroom. As the temptation came, so also came deliverance, but David, unlike Joseph, chose personal gratification irrespective of the odds. So he fell into temptation.

Temptations come in various manners, shapes, or forms. Anyone and anything can be used to tempt God's children; wife, children, parents, friends, colleagues, neighbor, workers, employers, brothers, sisters even people you don't know. Every ungodly and unholy desire gives birth to sin. Some desires may be godly but the avenue to achieving them will be ungodly, it's still sin. A man was preached to and he desired to worship and serve God. He attended a church service the first time and **knowingly** left with someone else's bible (stealing). A Christian brother gave a testimony, to make the story - testimony-worthy, he knowingly injected an event that did not occur (lie). You volunteered at a church-organized event and reported late one day. You deliberately did not sign the time card, and when asked what time you arrived you stated an earlier time (Cheating). I heard of the story of a man who joined a church and told the pastor he would like to join the ushering department (Greeters), when asked why he chose the ushering department he told the pastor that he could greet very well and make people feel comfortable, he also claimed that he could hug very well. In less than two years in the church he left with another man's wife. What is your purpose?

Temptation is of the devil. God does not tempt His children. The bible says;

> "Let no man say when he is tempted, I am tempted of God: For God cannot be tempted with evil, neither tempted he any man"
>
> JAMES 1:13 (KJV).

But another version puts it this way;

> "When tempted, no one should say, "God is
> tempting me." For God cannot be tempted by
> evil, nor does he tempt anyone;"
>
> JAMES 1:13 (NIV)

It is the devil that tempts. He does that either by himself, or using another person whom you trust, or by presenting an irresistible situation to you. But when it looks too good to be true, pray about it and ask God for the spirit of discernment. If you are not sure then let it go because God will reward you even if it was to be true and a real opportunity that you misinterpreted. God knows you misinterpreted it in other not to bring reproach to His name. He will give you a greater reward.

If you could not discern and you succumbed, it's a sin. But if you could not discern and let it go, not falling into it, you have not sinned even though you lost an opportunity. It is better to let an opportunity slide and you remain clean before God than grab an "opportunity" that later turns out to be a temptation. You may say "but God understands that 'I thought' it was an opportunity knocking at my door," that is why David said *"Teach me good discernment and knowledge, for I believe in Your commandments."* Psalm 119:66. You must ask God to teach you, and you must be willing to subject yourself to His command. He has given us divers spirits, including the spirit of discernment. 1 Corinthians

12:4-11. A writer once wrote "When it comes to the gift of discerning spirits, every born-again believer has a certain amount of it, which increases as the believer matures in the Spirit". You cannot already make up your mind before going to Him, you must let His will be done. Some people decide what to do already before going to God in prayers, and when God does not speak what they intend to hear, they disobey. *"He who keeps the law is a discerning son, But he who is a companion of gluttons humiliates his father."* Proverbs 28:7.

We are told that as we mature physically beyond the stage of drinking milk to cracking bones, so we also mature spiritually from knowing nothing to having the ability to discern good from evil, but it's by constantly remaining on the side of God, and being faithful. The bible says *"for everyone who lives on milk is unskilled in the word of righteousness, since he is a child. But solid food is for the mature, for those who have their powers of discernment trained by constant practice to distinguish good from evil."* Hebrews 5:13-14.

Remember, an ungodly desire, when pursued, will no doubt lead to sin. A desire that suddenly come across a tempting moment will no doubt lead to sin. But be watchful for the Lord is able to deliver us from all sights of evil if we ask, and if we are willing to say "NO" to sin.

WHEN SIN IS FULLY GROWN,
IT BRINGS FORTH DEATH

Sin has been, and will continue to be a hindrance to the relationship between us and God. This is not an accident. The God we serve cannot stand sin. God's *"… eyes are too pure to look on evil; you cannot tolerate wrongdoing..."* Habakkuk 1:13. Sin can bring down the good work of generations just as righteousness can lift the nation up. *"Righteousness exhorts a nation; But sin is a reproach to any people"* Proverbs 14:34. It is sin that separated us from the plan, purpose and the relationship God intended for us when Adam and Eve fell at the Garden of Eden. Since then, sin has become part of man's life and it is only God that can, and has saved us from it when He gave his only begotten son, Jesus Christ, to die and redeem our souls from destruction.

WHEN IS SIN FULLY GROWN?

Conception of sin is the beginning of the process. That conception of evil in itself is sin; it does not necessarily need to have been executed for it to amount to sin. To drive this home, I will draw analogies from a legal perspective; offences; solicitation, preparation, attempt, and perpetration.

SOLICITATION: This is when someone is enticing, advising, urging, inducing, encouraging, or inciting somebody else to perpetrate his own crime or felony, or to breach the peace of the land or any community either for a benefit or for nothing at all. The offence is committed the moment the initiator of the crime begins to tell the other person what that other person is being requested to do. Simply put, when there is a conspiracy. Once the crime/offence is mentioned, with or without the benefit, it becomes a complete crime/offence. But a conception of it is not a crime so long as it is just within you. Unlike solicitation, conception of sin is a sin in itself. Proverbs 15:26 says, *"The thoughts of the wicked are an abomination to the* LORD, *but gracious words are pure."* The thought alone, the conception of evil is forbidden by God. Mathew 5:28 says, *"… everyone who **looks** at a woman with lustful intent has already committed adultery with her in his heart."*

The thought of sin, any evil, or bad act is a sin by God's standard because God cannot stand sin and anything that looks like it. In solicitation, thinking about it is not a crime because the thinker may change his/her mind and not solicit anyone, but thinking about it is sin to God.

PREPARATION: This happens when there has been solicitation, and preparation to further the solicitation, e.g.

where someone solicited another to burn down a neighbor's house, and that other person went to the store to buy a gas container, a lighter and further bought gasoline at the gas station, clearly, an element of **preparation** can be established. That person could be charged with both crimes. If he's able to prove in the court that he acquired those items for a different purpose, fine. While mere thinking of preparation alone may not be a crime because no human being can read the mind of another person, preparation to commit sin is already a sin because the thought of it alone has made it sin even if you don't carry out the evil you thought about.

ATTEMPT: This is when the evil thought about has been attempted. It is an intention to bring about a criminal or a felonious result and a significant overt act in furtherance of the intention. Luckily for the **born-again** neighbor, as soon as the perpetrator ran away, there came a mighty wind that blew away the fire such that it only burnt one of the six legs holding the porch. An attempt was made to set the neighbor's house on fire, but God was watching over him and his home. But if the guy had not gone to the neighbor's house or if he had gone for a different purpose, maybe to survey the surrounding, the crime of attempt could not have been proved. Unlike attempt, before preparation, before attempt, sin is already established by thinking about it in the first instance.

PERPETRATION: This is when the neighbor's house or a substantial part of it actually caught fire and burnt down. A crime has been committed with clear evidence. This is no longer just a sin but also a crime.

While specific elements are needed, or certain stage have to be attained before conviction in any and all of the above four elements of inchoate crime/offence, in spiritual matters on the other hand, God, the ultimate judge, does not need a proof because He alone knows the heart of every man. *"I the* LORD *search the heart and test the mind, to give every man according to his ways, according to the fruit of his deeds."* Jeremiah 17:10.

He already knew from the beginning when the thought came into the heart of the perpetrator. Of course, He knows the end from the beginning and therefore knows how that thought was going to end, hence He does not want us to conceive evil against anyone.

If a sin is sin at the very thought of it, when then is a sin fully grown? A sin is fully grown when the proposed end result is achieved. Still using the above example, a sin that started with a thought and ended up in perpetration is fully grown when the neighbor's house was burnt down. Following the quote in Mathew 5:28 about he who looks at a woman with lust, the sin will be fully grown when he ends up committing adultery/fornication with that woman. This is why God will even punish the thought of evil or sin in our hearts because what is conceived in the heart, if not cautioned, often ends in disaster – great fall. Matthew 15:19 says, *"For out of the heart come evil thoughts--murder, adultery, sexual immorality, theft, false testimony, slander."* Also see Mark 7:21.

All sins begin from the heart; (1) what we say; *"… out of the abundance of the heart the mouth speaks"* Matthew 12:34; (2) what we do; *"A good man out of the good treasure of the heart bringeth forth good things: and an evil man out of the evil treasure bringeth forth evil things."* Matthew 12:35. The seat of sin is the heart. When we don't imagine it, sin presents itself into our thoughts even in our times of perfect dealings. That is why Apostle Paul says, *"… when I want to do good, evil is present with me."* Romans 7:21. In Ecclesiastes, there is a presentation that the heart of men is not only tainted with sin but filled with sin *"the hearts of all people are full with evil, and there is madness in their hearts during their lives – then they die"* Ecclesiastes 9:3. In fact, Jesus explains the hearts of men this way;

> "But the things that come out of a person's mouth come from the heart, and these defile them. For out of the heart come evil thoughts— murder, adultery, sexual immorality, theft, false testimony, slander. These are what defile a

person; but eating with unwashed hands does not defile them."

MATTHEW 15:18-20

Many thoughts take place in the heart; the good, the bad, and the ugly. A performance of any of those thoughts brings it to its fullness. Therefore, it would have been easier to explain that while a sin conceived exposes one to judgment, a sin that is fully grown – completely executed, brings death. But this is not so, for the bible says, *"the soul that sinneth, it shall die..."* Ezekiel 18:20. Whether a sin is merely conceived, or fully grown, it's a sin. Just as there is no small or big sin in the eyes of God, it also does not matter what was used in committing the sin; be it your mouth – use of curse words, profanity, ungodly conversations, slanderous acts, gossiping, bullying or your heart – as in the thought of evil, desiring evil, thinking of revenge; or your eyes – occupying yourself with pornographic materials, watching sexually explicit movies/magazines, looking lustfully; or your hand(s) - stealing, setting traps for others, libelous acts, fighting, poisoning; or doing anything that God distaste. Sin is sin. The price of any sin is death. The economic situation has not changed the value, the strength or weakness of any country's currency has not affected it, the movement of industries from one country to another has not affected it,

"For the wages of sin is death; but the gift of God is eternal life through Jesus Christ our Lord." Romans 6:23.

WHO ARE THE SINNERS?

Every one of us became sinners by reason of the disobedience of Adam and Eve in the Garden of Eden, and we all have their DNA flowing through our veins. *"just as sin entered the world through one man, and death through sin, and in this way death came to all people, because all sinned"* Romans 5:12. But, thank God for Jesus. When we become born again, the blood of Jesus washes us clean and makes us whole again; it takes away the Adamic DNA that existed in us as sinners that would have caused us to die eternal death, and gives us grace to be called the sons of God. We are born sinners. We become sinners immediately we get conceived by our mothers. David said, *"Surely I was sinful at birth, sinful from the time my mother conceived me."* Psalm 51:5. There is none that is holy for it is only the grace of God and by the death and resurrection of Jesus Christ that we are redeemed. Romans 3:23 says, *"for all have sinned and fall short of the glory of God."* It says ALL; that includes you and me. The book of Ecclesiastes says, *"Surely there is not a righteous man on earth who does good and never sins."* Ecclesiastes 7:20.

A writer once wrote that from Genesis to Revelation, the

Bible is clear that each one of us is responsible for our own actions. We reap what we sow and we sow the death penalty by all rights. Because we are sinners, the bible says we must die. Not just the physical death as we know it but the loss of eternity. Thank God for there shall be judgment after death (Hebrews 9:27), which gives believers a hope for eternity if we make it to heaven with Christ in us.

> "To them God has chosen to make known among the Gentiles the glorious riches of this mystery, which is Christ in you, the hope of glory."
>
> COLOSSIANS 1:27

God created us in His own image and likeness, after which He breathed His breath into us. He created us for a purpose – to worship Him, to glorify Him, and to enjoy His presence. Surely, He did not create us to be destroyed by any means. Hence, though Adam and Eve fell at the Garden of Eden where man lost fellowship with God, it wasn't His desire for us to perish, so He resolved to win us back to Himself. But for the God that He is, He gave us liberty to choose whom to follow/serve.

> "And if it seems evil unto you to serve the Lord, choose you this day whom ye will serve;

whether the gods which your fathers served that were on the other side of the flood, or the gods of the Amorites, in whose land ye dwell: but as for me and my house, we will serve the Lord."

JOSHUA 24:15

Remember, we are responsible for our actions. Though God gave us the liberty to choose whom to serve, our actions have consequences. This brings us to the topic of DEATH, the punishment for sin.

DEATH – THE PUNISHMENT FOR SIN

God said we should have no other gods before Him (Exodus 20:3), He said He is a jealous God (Exodus 20:5), He said we should not bow down before any other god, or serve them (Exodus 20:5), He said we should abstain from all appearance of evil (1 Thessalonians 5:22), He said the soul that sins shall surely die (Ezekiel 18:20). These are clear instructions given to all, whether you believe it or not. And He expects us to obey Him. He said if you love me, keep/obey my commandments (John 14:15). Anyone that is jealous will do anything and everything to get back at his/her offender if what that offender did is so painful and hurting, so is God. But in God's case, He just made it clear that if you disobey Him, it's sin, and the soul that sin shall die. For an unbeliever, everyone will die anyway.

Everyone will die but the bible says after death comes judgment (Hebrews 9:27). Yes, everyone will die and yes everyone will face judgment and what will the verdict be? There will be some that will die and go further to live their lives in eternity, while some will be cast into the lake of fire. *"Anyone whose name was not found written in the book of life was thrown into the lake of fire."* Revelation 20:15, where they will be tormented forever and ever.

God desired to win us back hence He sent His only son to come and die for our sin. *"For God so loved the world, that He gave His only begotten Son, that whosoever believe in Him SHOULD not perish, but have everlasting life."* John 3:16 (my emphasis).

Jesus came to die for believers; for those who proclaim the Kingship of God, and Jesus Christ as the one and only true son of God. He came for the remission of our sins, he came to reconcile us unto God, the father. His coming will greatly benefit all believers, whether they are dead or alive for He is the God of the dead and the God of the living.

> "For whether we live, we live unto the Lord;
> and whether we die, we die unto the Lord:
> whether we live therefore, or die, we are the
> Lord's. For to this end Christ both died, and

rose, and revived, that he might be Lord, both of the dead and living."

ROMANS 14:8-9

Those who die in Christ will be raised from the dead (raptured), while those who die as unbelievers will be thrown into the lake of fire (eternal condemnation). The bible puts it this way;

"Brothers and sisters, we do not want you to be uninformed about those who sleep in death, so that you do not grieve like the rest of mankind, who have no hope. For we believe that Jesus died and rose again, and so we believe that God will bring with Jesus those who have fallen asleep in him. According to the Lord's word, we tell you that we who are still alive, who are left until the coming of the Lord, will certainly not precede those who have fallen asleep. For the Lord himself will come down from heaven, with a loud command, with the voice of the archangel and with the trumpet call of God, and the dead in Christ will rise first. After that, we who are still alive and are left will be caught up together with them in the clouds to meet the Lord in the air. And so we will be with the Lord forever. Therefore, encourage one another with these words."

1 THESSALONIANS 4:13-18

Of a truth we are all sinners, for no one is perfect but God. Today, it may look like there is no difference between believers and unbelievers beside the fact that there is hope for believers, but on the day of resurrection the difference will be clear as to who gets raptured and who gets cast into the lake of fire for eternal condemnation. It will be risky to wait and see where the difference lies because on the said day, there will be no second chance any more. Now is the time! No one knows what tomorrow will bring.

Chapter Four
IN EVERY DECISION

It is therefore necessary to consider the word of God and see if our intended decision is in line with the word/will of God.

It is for a purpose that God created man: to have fellowship with man; for there to be a communion, closeness, intimacy with man. If then there was a purpose for God to have created man, it is wisdom that every man should seek God's consent to know if the next step he is about to take will fall in line with God's plan. This is one thing that Adam did not consider before accepting and eating that apple at the Garden of Eden. If you are an employee of a company, before you bind the company with any obligation you will have to find out from the Chief Executive Officer (CEO), or the board to know if such obligation is in line with the operations and policies of the company. If you don't and you are not privileged to enter such obligation, you are on your own. You take whatever comes out of it. More so, when your boundary has been defined, you are not permitted to go beyond it.

Adam and Eve had a boundary and they went beyond it; it does not matter what their excuses were. If we blame them every now and then for the sin they bestowed on us, Jesus Christ has given us a second chance, what are we doing with it? Therefore, since God made us for His own purpose, it is expedient and very important that in every decision we are about to make/take, there is every need to seek the face of God. If not for any other reason but to see if such decision is in line with God's plan and purpose for us or our family, or for our ministry. There is no need to mess up a second time.

In the days after Adam and Eve were created, after God had commanded them not to eat from that particular fruit in the middle of the garden, the bible records that Adam and Eve heard God coming and they went to hide because at this time, they had eaten of the fruit (sin of disobedience), and they discovered that they were naked - Genesis 3:8. Certain decisions we take may please us but they offend God. That is why it is important to seek the face of God in anything we do. God cannot behold sin neither can He have fellowship with a sinner. The decision we take can either draw us more to God or pull us farther away from Him. If we sin, God stays away from us because He said darkness has no business with light.

Though we may derive certain satisfaction from our action, but it's important to think deep if it's the will of God. One thing that should guide us as we make progress in our spiritual journey is to always ask ourselves when we are at a crossroad concerning certain decision: "what will Jesus do at times like this?" Of cause, to know what Jesus will do you must have to know Jesus. Take a clue from this; anything that is good is of God:

> "Everything good comes from God. Every perfect gift is from him. These good gifts come down from the Father who made all the lights in the sky…"
>
> JAMES 1:17

This may take us a little bit backward to the hearing of that still voice that helps us to determine whether what we are about to do is good or bad. That voice is there but it is left for us to either obey that which is good or take the easiest and more comforting route which is usually the easiest thing to do, but that route leads to destruction.

An armed robber will conceive in his heart to carry out a robbery operation, an adulterer conceived to commit adultery, a liar many times planned to lie, a person planned to cheat, an offended person plans a revenge, to take a colleague's job is planned etc. There is that still voice saying "this is not good," "it is a sin," "there will be a repercussion," (an unwanted consequence occurring sometime after an event or an action). There is however, another voice which may not really be sounding louder and clearer but because it speaks to what you already have in mind; that negative voice simply gained the upper hand. For a person who really fears God, he/she will ask "what will Jesus do in this situation?" If you really know God, you will know the right thing to do because you must have read in the bible, or you may have been told that "thou shall not steal," that lying is a sin, that you should not avenge for yourself for God says "vengeance is mine"

> "It is mine to avenge; I will repay. In due time
> their foot will slip; their day of disaster is near
> and their doom rushes upon them."
>
> DEUTERONOMY 32:35

In all decisions, in as much as it is necessary to consider the will of God (God's plan) for our lives at that moment, let's consider it along the following lines; I'm about to decide on certain issues, and since God made me for His own benefit how will that decision benefit Him? Does that decision align with the word of God? Is that decision taken at the right time – by God's standard? Did God approve of the action?

Will God change His mind after approval? If everything were in line with the word of God, how come I did not succeed?

How Will It Benefit (glorify) God?

Majorly, decisions we take in life especially as adults tend to have benefits in four areas: (1) financial benefits demand financial responsibilities; (2) employer/employee benefits demand respect, honor, and responsibilities to the employer/employee; (3) to benefit from your family, there should be a responsibility owed to the family; and (4) to benefit from God, there must be a commitment to the things of God and obedience to His command. There will be times when such decisions may be so difficult to make; where it does not bother on doing right or wrong. There might also be circumstances that may have to do with morality.

The Israelites were at a point like this when they were admonished by Moses in the book of Deuteronomy as follows:

> "I call heaven and earth as witnesses today
> against you, that I have set before you, life and
> death, blessing and cursing; therefore, choose
> life, that both you and your descendants may
> live; that you may love the LORD your God,

that you may obey His voice, and that you may cling to Him."

DEUTERONOMY 30:19-20

Abram obeyed God when God told him to leave his country, his people, and his father's house to a place where He will show him, Abram DECIDED to obey. How many people just leave their place of comfort to a place they don't know about, relying only on the leading of God. It might be possible today because we have Abraham as an example, but Abraham did not have anyone to look up to and say well, if this person did it I can do it. That decision glorified the name of the Lord, it benefited God, and so God did not only bless Abraham with Isaac through Sarah, He also made him father of many nations. Today, we are beneficiaries.

Moses was minding his business, taking care of his father-in-law's flock when suddenly, in the middle of nowhere in the bush, he saw a bush burning. Not only that the bush was burning but it was not being consumed. After all the conversations that went on between God and Moses, Moses DECIDED to work with God and gave himself up to be used. For this decision that later led to the freedom of the Israelites from the hands of Pharaoh and the Egyptians, God's name was glorified (benefit to God). God worked miracles through Moses, and He was with him all the time; in times of war and in times of peace.

Joseph, for the fear of God and respect for his master, Potiphar, he refused to sleep with Potiphar's wife. Though the master believed his wife when he put Joseph in Prison, the bible says "... *the* LORD *was with him; he showed him kindness and granted him favor in the eyes of the prison warden.*" Genesis 39:21 and "*The warden paid no attention to anything under Joseph's care, because the* LORD *was with Joseph and gave him success in whatever he did.*" Genesis 39:23. Joseph DECIDED not to sleep with his master's wife. It was a decision that glorified the name of God who had a plan for his future, and that was a decision that benefited God, it exalted the name of God.

There are decisions we make/take that, if in line with the will and purpose of God, they will glorify the name of the Lord. The decision to become born again – it will not just benefit you but those that you may directly or indirectly lead to God. The decision to help out somebody on the street, the decision to feed the hungry, the decision to preach the gospel, the decision to give godly counsel, the decision to help the needy, the decision to be truthful no matter what, the decision to give a lift in your car, the decision to pay for somebody's food, the decision to take somebody to church or a gospel event, etc. These are worthy decisions because someone else can decide to do the direct opposite; so which side are you on.

When you consider that your action will benefit God,

consider other points to be discussed below and move on in the right direction.

DOES IT ALIGN WITH GOD'S WORD/WILL?

Since we agree that there is a purpose that we need to fulfill on earth – the purpose for our creation, and haven learnt earlier that it is important to seek the face of God before we make/take decisions, it is therefore necessary to consider the word of God and see if our intended decision is in line with the word/will of God.

Following the word/will of God means going to Him in emptiness of heart. By this I mean you should not have a plan already laid out before going to God in prayer, that is a reverse order. Many people have missed it by going this way. When they pray after making plans and even if the spirit of God is telling them ANYTHING contrary, they won't listen and they will not hear because they have spent some time planning according to their own desire. Jesus said *"He must become greater; I must become less."* John 3:30. This simply means that we have to go to God empty, not nursing an idea. For His will to come to pass we must not have a set decision before going to God. Otherwise, there might be conflict. Let the will of God be done, and when you submit to that will He will give you wisdom to follow through.

Any decision that is not in line with the will of God is not God's. Most issues of life have guidance in the word of God. What makes some decisions difficult is the purpose: will your purpose please God? There are two things to a purpose; what is your purpose for doing or going to do what you are intending, what will be the later end of your action? Most times, our actions do not end in the primary purpose for which we acted. A man had a desire to serve in the church and registered to be a worker in the Ushering ministry, in less than two years he left the church with another man's wife. Probably he did not have that intention from the beginning but temptation came in and the devil altered the purpose. That is why it is very important to thrust all our decisions into the hands of God. Pray for His leading, and His protection against all manners of evil.

Some people become pastors, ministers, priests, deacons/deaconesses, workers for different reasons. Some may have good intentions but certainly not all. What is your purpose for doing what you do in the church today? Is it solely to please God, to obey His command, to do His will, or is it partly God and partly you? Some people go to church to identify with "a group," to hide under a church, to be called a Christian. Some go to church to create a customer base for their trade, some, to boost their social status. Remember, the reason why Jesus Christ scattered the temple in Matthew 21. He said *"It is written,"* he said to them, *"'My house will be called a house of prayer,' but you are making it 'a den of robbers."* Matthew 21:13. This simply means that instead of serving God for God's purpose(s), we are "serving God" for personal benefit/gain/profit, which does not align with the word of God.

IS THIS THE RIGHT TIME?

The bible says in Ecclesiastes 3:1-8 that "there is a time for everything, and a season for every activity under the heavens: a time to be born and a time to die, a time to plant and a time to uproot, a time to kill and a time to heal, a time to tear down and a time to build, a time to weep and a time to laugh, a time to mourn and a time to dance, a time to scatter stones and a time to gather them, a time to embrace and a time to refrain from embracing, a time to search and a time to give up, a time to keep and a time to throw away, a time to tear and a time to mend, a time to be silent and a time to speak, a time to love and a time to hate, a time for war and a time for peace. This follows therefore that there is an appropriate time even in the decisions we make. It is therefore important that even when we dream, when we aspire, when we visualize, it is still necessary to ask God if this is His will, and if convinced, is this the right time?

There are some great ideas that have failed because

they were executed at the wrong time. During the 2008 presidential election in the U.S., I saw a documentary where a state senator advised the then Senator Barack Obama to hold on to his ambition of running for the presidency, and when he perceived the environment ripe enough he told him "this is the time." Barack Obama ran and won the election.

God is not an author of confusion, ask Him for a right time, and obey. A baby born today does not start walking, and certainly does not start running at the very first step. Life is in stages, and achievements come over time.

One thing we have to understand is that our time is not God's time, a thousand days in the eyes of men is like a second in God's eyes. What God cares about is that whatever He promised He will bring to pass, when and how is not for us to decide.

WILL GOD CHANGE HIS MIND?

There are three kinds of situation here; a decision that will benefit God – when God want you to do something for His sole benefit, like when He told Abraham to sacrifice Isaac; a decision of mutual benefit – when God asked Moses to go get the Israelites out of Egypt; a decision that solely benefit us – when we pray for protection, breakthrough, forgiveness etc.

The LORD Almighty has sworn, "Surely, as I have

planned, so it will be, and as I have purposed, so it will happen. Isaiah 14:24. This is when we make ourselves available. But when we act like we don't hear God speaking, He is not going to be slowed down because of our inactivity. In fact, God said "I tell you, if they keep quiet, the stones will cry out." Luke 19:40. This simply means that if we get a directive and we are convinced that it is of God, and then decide to push it aside, God can raise somebody else to do it. It's the same thing even if it's our own personal ambition.

Moses felt the pain the Israelites were passing through in Egypt, hence he was the right person God could use to bring them out of Egypt. If Moses had not made himself available, God would have still use somebody else.

God does not change His mind unless when we are not available. If it's a purpose for God's own or for mutual benefit, God will use someone else, but where it's for our own sole benefit and we refuse to act, He may let it go unless He really want to use you. Jonah did not have a choice but to go to Nineveh. Jonah 3.

Chapter Five

SOME DECISIONS I HAVE MADE

In a church that has close to one hundred youths (maybe more), not more than five were always in attendance in church activities and youth meetings. One thing I did not do was to walk away, but what I did was to see none attendance as an area I was needed to work on

Like many today's successful, and some not too successful ministers of God, I was not born into a Christian home. At an early age, I had a cousin who was taking me to a nearby Baptist Church where I first got a feel of "Church-going" like many kids today. But after that cousin left our family house, I did not go to church any more until after a long time when a tenant moved into my father's house. This new tenant will take us to church every Sunday, even made for us (Kids) what we called "garment" depending on the group you joined. I was always looking forward to Sundays because I will have to wear my near "garment" to (as I later got to know it) a Cherubim and Seraphim Church. Soon afterwards, the tenant left town on transfer because he was in the military, we then joined another branch of the church after a period of time. There, I joined the Choir at age 10, but because this was predominantly "the kids' affairs," in a non-Christian home, I had to stop. I never went to church again until after a very long time.

When you have a desire to serve God, and you are not in a position to decide for yourself what to and not to do – simply because when you are still dependent on others, only time will tell, though it might be delayed.

When I gained a little independence, I became a yearly worshipper because I had not been to church in a very long time. I only went to church when one of my brothers (now deceased) was in town. We will go to church together; he will make me do morning devotions with him. Most times he will give me the scripture reading for the day and ask me to read it to myself and he will do his reading too. At the end he will ask me "what will you pick as a focus for today?" Coincidentally, what I picked most of the time was what he also had in mind. We would pray (sometimes he prayed and some other times I did), and he will always tell me "you are going to be a pastor." To me I was just obeying him as an elder brother because when he leaves town, all "that pastor thing" will end. When he stopped coming as frequently as it used to be, I became a yearly worshipper. I sneaked into the church on New Year's Eve at about 11:50 – 11:55 p.m. after partying, with the purpose of entering the New Year inside the church. Some people still do it today, even in America. I see them and smile. I have preached about it using myself as an example, and I pray they will find Christ one of these nights. On December 31st 1996, I went in as usual but came out a new person. That was my first major spiritual decision.

Gradually, I began to discover the God I walked away from many years ago. I'm sure He knew it was not my fault, and this time I have to prove it wasn't my fault because I did not have any reason now not to serve Him. I started learning everything afresh. The day I bought my first bible, I received a monetary gift double the amount I spent. I created study times and learnt to pray again. A beloved brother (whom I used to think was bothering me) drew me to the youth fellowship, though it took him a long time to convince me but he never gave up on me. At the youth fellowship, I struggled to remain because as a new convert attendance was very discouraging. In a church that had close to one hundred youths (maybe more), not more than five were always in attendance. One thing I did not do was to walk away, but what I did was to see non-attendance as an area I was needed to serve. I later became faithful in the youth fellowship – another decision I made and did not waiver.

Towards the end of that year, I was made the fellowship's Vice President. It's God's work, I never said "No" unless much later which I will also talk about. If He needs me for his assignment, why not? At this time I was also in school and residing in the hostel. One Tuesday evening, I decided to pay a visit to the youth fellowship in town even though I was also committed at my campus fellowship. I was surprised that the fellowship's attendance had not changed. That day, I **decided** I will never miss fellowship again. So I would leave for school on Monday morning, come back to attend fellowship on Tuesday and return to campus on Wednesday. Another decision I made was to try and make a difference. I did this for a while until it was time to choose a new set of leaders. Coincidentally, I was sent out of town for a six-week course. I was there when I received a call that I have been chosen as the new youth president. I give God all the glory for what He did with me, a position that prepared me for where I am today.

With the good leaders God gave me on my team, and with God on our side, we were able to turn the fellowship fully around to the glory of God. I am sure that a lot of lives were touched during that period, there was a transformation. I had only spent a few months when I was transferred out of town, but God helped us and we did not lose focus. But shortly afterwards, I returned back from transfer and I was made the youth zonal coordinator. The zone had about 109 branches which overwhelmed me, but again, I did not say "No". I decided to take this position believing that God was on my side. I was in my final year as a law student, working full time, and just got married with a son. I had every reason to have run away from that position, but I allowed God to take control. As a zonal coordinator, I was seconding as State Deputy Coordinator too. Everything went so well. That year we had the very first and very successful State Youth Convention, and the following year we had the very first and successful Youth Zonal Conference.

When you let God use you, He will strengthen you. He will grant you wisdom and all that is necessary for you to succeed. He makes use of the available and he who is willing to do His work. *I am a testimony that God does not owe His workers, and He pays in the highest currency.* When I sit down some times and look back, many times I cannot even imagine how we did all that we did. I am not surprised today that many of the people we worked together then have become ministers too; some have become church founders and doing very well. In 2004, God relocated me and my family to the United States in a way He alone could – one of the dividends of our work with Him.

In the United States, I have worked with and for God in various capacities to the best of my ability. The only time

I have said "No" to any responsibility in the church since I became born again was when I was called to go pastor a church, because with churches these days…, I wasn't sure if that was what I really want to do. I had to seek the face of God and like Gideon (Judges 6:36-40), God has to prove to me that this was what He wanted me to do. After refusing that call for about four years, certain things happened that scared me. It wasn't in the most convenient time; there wasn't going to be any personal benefit but every reason why I should not do it (based on my own assessment and personal comfort). I got scared of situations around me, but I heard God reminding me that He has taken me through more difficult times. I asked for two proofs as a confirmation to span a period of two years, the first one came to pass very quickly, and on the seventeenth month the second confirmation came to pass in a very big way.

Decisions must have the hands of God in them. If it's His will, no matter the forces that may be against you, God will grant you victory. In all my journeys till this point, I have had challenges but the good part is that one with God is majority. Becoming a parish pastor has not been different; I faced challenges from the very most unexpected sources, but I kept moving on. Life's journey is not all smooth as Jesus already gave a warning ahead of time. In all your dealings, trust God and not man, because that person you think is going to stand by you in the day of trouble may be the person who will push you into trouble. God says *"call upon my name in the day of trouble, and I will deliver you..."* Psalm 50:15. He has always been my guard and my guide, I will forever praise His name. I will forever worship Him. I will always honor Him. I will always look unto Him. *"I will lift up mine eyes unto the hills, from whence cometh my help. My help cometh from the* LORD, WHICH MADE HEAVEN AND EARTH." Psalm 121:1-2.

If you are in the middle of a situation this moment, be encouraged to put God first. Seek His face with a clean heart, believe He can and will answer you. Trust in Him all the way and do not depend or lean on your own understanding. Enemies will scare you, they will threaten you directly and/or indirectly, but if you believe in Him, just let Him lead the way.

One thing that has made me strong, and even stronger these past few years is looking at what God has done for me in the past, and the fact that He's still alive to do it again because He does not change. He has been my guard and He will always be so long as I bring myself under His subjection. *"The LORD is my strength and my shield; my heart trusts in him, and he helps me. My heart leaps for joy, and with my song I will praise him."* Psalm 28:7. If you make God your companion, your team lead, your ever present help in times of need, He is faithful to see you through.

Chapter Six
CONCLUSION

Recently, a very close relative of mine said something I really believe is true. She said each time she thinks about all that God has done for her within the short period she has known Him, she regrets not knowing Him early enough. That is an acknowledgement from a grateful heart. I think like that many times too.

The Psalmist says *God hath spoken once; twice have I heard this; that power belong unto God.* Psalm 62:11. Whatever you have read in this book that may have interested you has not been by magic, neither was it by excellence. No amount of strength could have done it either. But by the grace and power of God. There is nothing we can accomplish without God, hence the bible says *"with God, nothing shall be impossible."* Matthew 19:26.

Beloved, God owns us, He created us for His purpose.

It is very important that in anything we do and in whatever decision we may be considering, it has to be the will of God. If we put God first, the journey is smoother and achievement is sure.

Many people forget God in their plans out of exigencies and emergencies, forgetting that they can only arrive if God journeys with them. God is a companion, He's a dependable ally, and the lifter of our heads. If we are in agreement that there's nothing we do that God does not know about, know also and believe that He knows every of our situation, and He will only take care of it if that situation is committed into His hands. He cannot mend our brokenness if we are still holding on to the pieces. Give Him the pieces and He will fix it for you.

God is the author and the finisher of our faith. Hebrews 12:2, the alpha and omega- Revelation 1:8, the first and the last- Revelation 22:13, the beginning and the end- Revelation 22:13.

Many people spend longer time in doing simple things because they went about it the wrong way, believing in themselves and not in God. This is not new at all, and it's not peculiar only to certain people.

The Israelites spent a much longer time getting to the Promised Land than they would have normally spent because they doubted God. They were to take possession of the land God had promised their forefathers, a land "flowing with milk and honey," Exodus 3:8. Prior to entering the Promised Land after they had gone to survey the land and its people, they became convinced they could not oust the current inhabitants of the land, even though God told them they could. Their lack of belief in God's word and promises brought forth the wrath of God. He cursed them with forty years of wandering in the wilderness until the unbelieving generation died off, never stepping foot onto the Promised Land. God does not like us distrusting Him, it is faithlessness.

God may sometimes rebuke us openly, at many other times, He expects us to know and obey His word. In the case of the Israelites, He said to Moses, "How long will they refuse to believe in me, in spite of all the miraculous signs I have performed among them? I will strike them down with a plague and destroy them" Numbers 14:11. But Moses intervened.

I hope you will find something informational, something transformational, something spiritual, and something educative in this book. Believe that if God spoke it, He can bring it to pass if you commit it into His hands. If you dreamt it, it is possible. Study His word (2 Tim. 2:15) to find His will and desire for your next move and see God working on your behalf.

BIBLIOGRAPHY

ALL bible references were KJV, ASV, ESV or NIV except where otherwise stated

Charles Pope: (Community in Mission) – What is temptation, why does God permit it, and what are its sources? March 22, 2015.

Worthy Watchman – An Answer to "What is the Spiritual Gift of Discerning Spirits? www.gotQuestions.org-discerning-spirits April 18, 2015

Why was Israel cursed with forty years of wilderness wandering? http://www.gotquestions.org/wilderness-wandering.html

Printed in the United States
By Bookmasters